Elegance

From

Within

UNLOCKING THE SECRETS

TO

GRACEFUL FEMININITY

By: LEAH LEWIS

ELEGANCE FROM WITHIN:

UNLOCKING THE SECRETS
TO
GRACEFUL FEMININITY

Published by Malkut Publishing.
For inquiries, please send an email to:
malkut.publishing@gmail.com.

Contents

Acknowledgments

To my mother Althea, you are my biggest supporter and dearest friend. Much of what I have written here, I have learned from you. Thank you for all that you are in my life.

To my brother Dwight, thank you for always being there for me and encouraging me. You are a wonderful big brother.

I love you both dearly.

To my Heavenly Father, You are my greatest inspiration and joy. Thank you for giving me this book to write. May it glorify You in every way, and guide the many women who will read it, along the path that You have set for them in this life.

A Note From the Author

Imagine a life where you exude a quiet confidence that turns heads the moment you step into a room— not because of flashy clothing or extravagant accessories, but because of the grace and charm that naturally radiate from within you. Picture yourself navigating life's twists and turns with poise, maintaining your composure even in the face of adversity, and inspiring admiration through your kindness and integrity. Elegance is not a privilege reserved for the wealthy or the famous; it is a quality that every woman can possess. It is a journey that begins on the inside of you, with the transformation of your heart, mind, and soul.

I want you to see that true elegance can be learned and developed, and once you discover your own unique path to elegance, there's no turning back.

Elegance will become a part of who you are and flow into every aspect of your life. From the way that you dress, to the way that you walk, the way that you speak and the things that you say, the way that you behave, and the way that you treat and interact with others. Everything changes. You begin to see yourself as a woman of value and treat yourself as such. Others begin to see your value, and esteem you more highly as well. This has been my experience becoming an elegant woman, and I know that it will be yours too.

This book is your personal guide to unlocking the timeless secrets of elegance and femininity. Together, we will explore what it truly means to live with grace, from developing an elegant mindset to nurturing your health and well-being. We will delve into the art of self-care, the power of emotional intelligence, and the strength that comes from having a deep relationship with God. You will discover how to embrace your unique beauty, enhance your style, and embody the feminine grace that inspires others to be their best selves, simply by you being your best self.

Through relatable stories, practical tips, and reflective exercises, I invite you to embark on a journey of self-discovery and transformation. By the end of the book, you will not only *look* elegant but also *feel* elegant, ready to make a positive impact in your life and the world around you. This is exactly what you've been looking for. Now, let's begin this beautiful journey of elegance and femininity together.

Chapter 1

The Essence of

Elegance

Chapter 1:

The Essence of Elegance

The Timeless Appeal of Elegance

What is elegance? Elegance is a concept of harmony and balance in your thinking, your appearance, your behaviour, and your environment. It is an enduring quality that transcends trends and time. Elegance has nothing to do with wealth or societal status, but is shown as an inner light that shines through the actions, words and presence of any woman, of any background. An elegant woman is like a breath of fresh air wherever she goes; she uplifts and inspires those around her with her grace, thoughtfulness, and dignity. True elegance is not about drawing attention to yourself but rather, about leaving a lasting impression on the world around you through your character.

Throughout history, elegant women have stood out not because of their outward beauty, but because of their inner qualities. Think of Audrey Hepburn, whose timeless style was matched only by her humility and humanitarian work, or Ruth from the Bible, whose loyalty and faithfulness made her a woman of great renown. These women remind us that elegance is as much about who you are as it is about what you do.

Inner Beauty as the Foundation.

Outer beauty may catch the eye, but inner beauty captures the heart. An elegant woman understands that her true worth lies not in her physical appearance, but in the values she upholds and the way she treats others. Inner beauty is generated through kindness, empathy, humility, and a steadfast sense of purpose. As 1 Peter 3:3-4 says, *"Do not let your adornment be merely outward—arranging the hair, wearing gold, or putting on fine apparel—rather let it be the hidden person of the heart, with the incorruptible beauty of a gentle and quiet spirit, which is very precious in the sight of God"* (NKJV).

How can you develop this inner beauty? Doing this requires being intentional about the effort being put into improving yourself. It involves reflecting on your character, identifying areas for growth, and actively seeking to align your thoughts and actions with your values. For instance, practising kindness can be as simple as offering a listening ear to a friend in need, or showing patience when someone tests your limits. Each act of inner beauty strengthens the foundation of your elegance.

True elegance radiates from a woman who has taken the time to nurture her inner world. You *must* do the inner work. Imagine walking into a room and instantly putting others at ease with your warmth and genuine interest in their well-being, not because you put on an act, but because you genuinely do care. This inner beauty is what makes an elegant woman unforgettable.

Femininity and Masculinity: The Balance Within

Now let us take a look at the characteristic that enhances our elegance as women - femininity. Every woman possesses both feminine and masculine traits, and true elegance lies in balancing these qualities. Femininity is often associated with nurturing, empathy, and gentleness, while masculinity reflects strength, assertiveness, and decisiveness. Femininity involves naturally *receiving* - for instance, compliments, gifts or assistance from others. Masculinity involves naturally *giving* - for instance, time, energy, money, assistance, gifts, or anything of value. Femininity involves *being*, whereas masculinity involves *doing*. Neither set of traits is superior; they complement each other and are essential for navigating life effectively.

Consider the example of a mother who embodies both qualities. Her femininity allows her to comfort and nurture her child, while her masculine traits enable her to set boundaries and protect her family. Similarly, an elegant woman knows when to be soft and when to stand firm, creating a harmonious balance that commands respect and admiration. As an elegant woman, you want to embrace your femininity wholly and be aware of when you are functioning too strongly with masculine energy.

Redefining Femininity in the Modern World

Modern society often misconstrues femininity as weakness or submissiveness, causing many women to become unnaturally hard, cold, aggressive, and detached from others, particularly from the graces shown by masculine men. However, true femininity is far from fragile. It is a profound source of strength, rooted in emotional intelligence, empathy, and inner confidence. True femininity will allow you to lead with compassion, influence with kindness, and inspire others through quiet strength and authenticity. It does not diminish your authority but enhances it, enabling you to connect with others on a deeply personal level.

The ability to balance both feminine and masculine qualities is what creates a fully empowered woman. While masculinity often emphasizes assertiveness, logic, and action, femininity highlights intuition, empathy, and collaboration. Again, both are essential, and when harmonized, they allow a woman to approach life with wisdom and grace. A truly elegant woman understands how to draw on both aspects, standing firm in her values while caring for those around her with tenderness and love.

Society often praises strength in its most visible, outward forms, such as career achievements or physical power, while overlooking the quiet resilience of femininity. Yet the strength of a woman who endures, uplifts, and inspires is profound and transformative. Think of the courage it takes to lead a family, sustain friendships, or offer forgiveness in the face of hurt. True femininity is a beacon of grace under pressure, showing that resilience can be soft yet unyielding. You can be very much feminine, yet ever so strong.

Balancing Strength and Grace

To achieve this balance between the feminine and masculine energies, it helps to reflect deeply on your strengths and areas for growth. Self-awareness is key to cultivating harmony between them both. Consider moments when you might shy away from asserting yourself due to fear of conflict or rejection. Do you avoid expressing your opinions in professional settings because you fear being perceived as overly aggressive? Or perhaps you suppress your softer, warmer side in an attempt to appear as being strong and self-sufficient. Do you find yourself doing this often?

Acknowledging these tendencies is the first step toward personal growth. By recognizing both your assertive and receptive qualities, you can begin to integrate them more effectively. For instance, an elegant woman can lead a business meeting with clarity and confidence while still showing empathy and active listening to her team. She can set firm boundaries in relationships without sacrificing kindness and grace.

Practical ways to balance strength and grace include *practising active listening*, where you fully engage with others' perspectives before responding. You listen to understand,

and allow others to feel heard. You do not listen to argue or shut down others' ideas or opinions. Another approach is *mindful communication*, where you express your thoughts clearly yet gently, ensuring that both honesty and compassion coexist. You are aware of your tone and the reaction that both what you say and how you say it can arouse. *Journaling* can also be a powerful tool for you to explore moments when you've felt either too passive or overly forceful, helping you to identify patterns and areas for refinement. Identify what may be causing you to behave the way that you do, whether it's your home or work environment, unhealed hurts from the past, deep-rooted insecurity, or overwhelm from current circumstances.

Ultimately, a balanced woman feels secure in her identity. She can embrace her nurturing, compassionate side without fear of being perceived as weak, just as she can assert her boundaries and ambitions without losing her softness. This harmony creates a magnetic presence, one that draws respect and admiration effortlessly. Is this the kind of woman that you see yourself becoming? Well, it's absolutely possible. Let's go bit further.

The Values That Define Elegance

At its core, elegance is a reflection of your personal values. Kindness, humility, godliness, and self-respect are foundational pillars that you will need to strengthen and focus on building.

Kindness not only lights up a room but also creates meaningful connections with others. It can be shown in simple yet powerful ways—offering a genuine compliment, being patient with a stranger, offering a helping hand to someone in need, or speaking words of encouragement to someone facing challenges, are all acts of kindness. The thing is, kindness may not always come naturally to everyone, but know that it's more than just a feeling. You truly must care, firstly in your thoughts, and then in your actions. You have to work on first *thinking* kindly of others, and only then can you genuinely demonstrate it out of the compassion that it creates in your heart.

Humility fosters respect and makes you approachable, ensuring that your presence is warm rather than intimidating. Humility helps you to see yourself as being equal, not higher than others, and so you treat others of every walk of life with the same respect that you would like to receive. It involves acknowledging your strengths without arrogance, but instead with gratitude, and celebrating the successes of others without jealousy or envy. A humble woman remains teachable, because she knows that she does not always have the answer, and she always seeks growth without needing validation or applause.

Godliness anchors you in your faith, knowing that there is someone greater than yourself whom you can trust to guide you through life's triumphs and trials. It provides a moral compass for your actions as you align your life with spiritual teachings and principles, and draw strength from having a relationship with God. A godly woman exudes love, grace, forgiveness, and integrity in her interactions, inspiring those around her to pursue higher standards of character. She respects herself and honours herself, as she sees herself as being valuable in God's eyes. We delve a little deeper into the importance of godliness in your elegant journey later on.

Self-respect allows you to set the standard for how others treat you and ensures that you honour your worth as a woman. People will treat you based on how you treat yourself, and on what you allow them to do or say to you. The way that you dress, groom yourself, speak, carry yourself and behave, whether privately or publicly, show a great deal of your level of self-respect. Self-respect also involves establishing healthy boundaries in relationships, refusing to settle for less than you rightly deserve, and maintaining dignity in all situations. A woman with self-respect values herself not only for her appearance or achievements, but for her intrinsic worth. You have to know that you are a person created with purpose and significance, and it's up to you to present the best version of yourself to the world around you.

Living by these values requires consistent effort and deliberateness. True kindness means choosing to be gentle and compassionate even when it feels inconvenient or unreciprocated. Humility involves celebrating your achievements without arrogance, understanding that your worth is inherent, not determined by accolades. Godliness calls for unwavering faith and standing firm in your beliefs despite societal pressures, while self-respect demands that you uphold boundaries and make decisions that align with your dignity and worth.

These values go beyond mere behaviour— they shape your thoughts and perceptions. Consider how you view others: Do you extend grace when someone makes a mistake, or do you judge them harshly? An elegant woman chooses to see the good in people, offering encouragement and understanding, rather than criticism. She fosters an inclusive mindset that uplifts and inspires, seeing herself as a vessel of positive influence in every interaction.

By developing these values internally, they will be naturally reflected in your outward presence. A woman who embodies kindness, humility, godliness, and self-respect becomes a beacon of elegance, inspiring those around her to rise to a similar standard. To reiterate, know that true elegance, after all, is not merely about appearance—it is the radiance of a beautiful heart shining through in all that you do.

Remember, your inner beauty only enhances your outer beauty. May you be inspired to cultivate the inner beauty and values that define you as the elegant woman you are.

Chapter 2

The Elegant Mindset

Chapter 2:

The Elegant Mindset

The Mindset of an Elegant Woman

Your mindset shapes your identity. Who you are and how you perceive your reality, stems from the thoughts that you focus on every day, whether positive or negative. What you think and believe about yourself influences how you interact with the world around you. For an elegant woman, this means generating thoughts that reflect your values and aspirations. It starts with understanding who you are: a daughter of

God, uniquely created with purpose and dignity. This foundational identity becomes the anchor for an elegant mindset.

From now on, you must not allow external situations to dictate your sense of worth. Your circumstances do not define you. Other people's opinions do not define you. Instead, take control of your inner world, that is, what you daily think about and focus on, choosing positive thoughts that uplift, empower, and inspire you to keep going. This is important because your mind cannot decipher between the truth and a lie, but believes what it is fed repeatedly. This is a fact. If you constantly tell yourself (or allow others to say to you) that you are not good enough, then that is what you will believe, and that is what will become your reality. On the other hand, if you repeatedly tell yourself that you are confident, brave or smart, for example, that is what you will believe and ultimately become. You must therefore be purposeful with what you feed your mind daily, carefully filtering out thoughts of insecurity, discouragement, regrets and harsh criticisms - things that do not truthfully define who you are. Choose instead to focus on what is true, noble, and praiseworthy, as you align your thoughts with your values, paving the way for a life filled with purpose and peace. As Philippians 4:8 advises: *"Finally, brethren, whatever things are true, whatever things are noble, whatever things are just, whatever things are pure, whatever things are lovely, whatever things are of good report, if there is any virtue and if there is anything praiseworthy—meditate on these things"* (NKJV). Developing this mindset will make a wonderfully positive difference in your life's journey.

Strategies for Gratitude and Positivity

Gratitude is a cornerstone of an elegant mindset. When you practice thankfulness, you shift your focus from what is lacking to what is abundant in your life. You take nothing for granted and recogise the significance of the blessings that come to you each day, no matter how seemingly simple. To actively train your mind to identify reasons to be grateful, you can begin by keeping a gratitude journal. Each day, jot down three things you are thankful for, whether it's a kind word from a friend, the beauty of a sunrise, or the gift of health. Over time, this practice transforms your outlook, making you more attuned to life's blessings.

Faith also plays a vital role in sustaining positivity. It's supremely important to believe that God is with you, for you and not against you. He *is* on your side. And so, trusting in His plan for your life frees you from the weight of worry and allows you to approach life with a sense of calm assurance. Consider the words of Jeremiah 29:11: *"'For I know the thoughts that I think toward you,' says the Lord, 'thoughts of peace and not of evil, to give you a future and a hope'"* (NKJV). This promise reminds us that no matter the circumstances that we may be facing, His plans for us are *good*, and that we are held in His loving care.

Positivity involves actively managing your thoughts. When negative or self-critical ideas arise, counter them with affirmations of truth and encouragement. You have to consciously fill your mind with faith. For instance, if you catch yourself thinking, "I'm not good enough," replace it with, *"I am fearfully and wonderfully made"* (Psalm 139:14). When you feel like something is too difficult to achieve, remind yourself, that *"I can do all things through Christ who strengthens me."* (Philippians 4:13), and that *"with God, all things are possible"* (Matthew 19:26). This practice not only uplifts your spirit but also reinforces your self-worth. It may be helpful to write out these and other scriptures and commit them to memory, so that you can draw on them when necessary. Place them somewhere visible, so that through repetition, you train your mind to believe for the good.

The Strength of Humility

Let's take another look at the rich, character-strengthening quality - humility. Humility is often misunderstood as weakness, but in reality, it is a profound strength. An elegant woman recognises her value without becoming prideful and acknowledges her imperfections without bringing herself down. She understands that she is not better than anyone else, and does not think of herself more highly than she should. Through humility you can celebrate others' successes, learn from your past mistakes, and remain open to growth. As the Scripture says in Philippians 2:3, *"Let nothing be done through selfish ambition or conceit, but in lowliness of mind [humility] let each esteem others better than himself"* (NKJV, emphasis added).

Consider the example of Queen Elizabeth II, who exemplified humility throughout her reign. Although holding her country's highest office, she consistently prioritised service over self-interest, earning respect and admiration worldwide. Despite her prestigious position as a monarch, her humble disposition made her relatable to her people, proving that true elegance lies in putting others at ease.

Humility also fosters meaningful relationships. It helps you to look past your own wants or needs, and focus on the well-being of others. When you approach others with a genuine interest in their thoughts, experiences, loved ones, or interests, you create an atmosphere of trust and respect. Humility also helps you to submit to authority, and give honour to whom it is due, whether to someone else of high or even low esteem, no matter your own status or position. This quality not only enhances your interactions but also strengthens your character.

The Power of Poise in Every Situation

Poise is all about your demeanour - how you carry yourself and conduct yourself. It is the ability to remain composed and graceful, no matter the circumstances. It is a hallmark of an elegant mindset and a skill that can be developed and become naturally ingrained into your actions, with purposeful practice. Imagine yourself in a tense meeting where emotions run high. Instead of reacting impulsively, you take a deep breath, collect your thoughts, and respond calmly. This display of poise not only diffuses tension but also elevates your presence.

To develop poise, practise mindfulness. Pay attention to your body language, tone of voice, and facial expressions. Are you conveying confidence and calmness, or do your actions reflect anxiety or aggression? Are you overly loud and boisterous, or do you consciously regulate your volume by speaking with a measured tone? Small adjustments, like maintaining steady eye contact or slowing down physical movement and gestures, can make a significant difference.

Poise also involves emotional regulation. When you feel overwhelmed, take a moment to centre yourself. Prayer and deep breathing are effective tools for finding balance. For example, reciting Joshua 1:9—*"Have I not commanded you? Be strong and of good courage; do not be afraid, nor be dismayed, for the Lord your God is with you wherever you go."* (NKJV)—can provide comfort and clarity in challenging moments.

Practical Exercises for an Elegant Mindset

To solidify the principles of an elegant mindset, incorporate these exercises into your daily routine:

1. **Morning Reflection:** Begin each day by meditating on a Bible verse or positive affirmation. For example, repeat, *"I am clothed with strength and dignity,"* as inspired by Proverbs 31:25, or "I am God's daughter, and deeply loved by my Father", or "God works all things together for my good", as inspired by Romans 8:28.

2. **Gratitude Journal:** Write down three things you are thankful for every evening or before bed. Reflect on how these blessings have enriched your day.

3. **Mindset Check-Ins:** Set aside moments throughout the day to assess your thoughts. Are they aligned with your values? If not, consciously redirect them.

4. **Poise Practice:** Role-play challenging scenarios, such as handling criticism or managing stress. Focus on maintaining composure and responding thoughtfully.

5. **Service Acts:** Perform small acts of kindness, such as complimenting a colleague or helping a neighbour. These gestures reinforce humility and gratitude.

By shaping your thoughts, embracing gratitude and humility, and cultivating poise, you lay a firm foundation for building and maintaining an elegant mindset. This chapter invites you to transform your inner world, empowering you to navigate life with grace and confidence. Be encouraged to re-read it as often as you need to, to help you stay on course for transforming your mindset for the good.

Chapter 3

Building Unshakable
Confidence

Chapter 3:

Building Unshakable Confidence

Confidence Without Arrogance

An elegant woman is a confident woman, yet confidence is often misunderstood. As women, many of us struggle to embrace our confidence out of fear that we may be perceived as being arrogant. This could not be further from the truth. True confidence is not about being boastful or self-centred; it is a quiet assurance rooted in self-awareness, humility, and grace. It is intentional *belief* in yourself, coupled with the ability to trust in your capabilities, and in the matchless capabilities of God. You also remain open to growth and learning. Confidence without arrogance is magnetic, drawing people to you because they sense your genuine strength and authenticity.

An elegant woman understands that confidence begins within. She knows that her value is not tied to her accomplishments, possessions, or social status, but to her intrinsic worth as a creation of God. Let this understanding liberate you from the need to compete with or compare yourself to other women, and allow yourself to walk into any room with composure and ease. For example, consider a scenario where you are meeting a group of strangers at a networking event. Confidence enables you to introduce yourself with warmth and sincerity, engaging others in meaningful conversations without seeking to dominate the interaction.

To develop confidence, start by reflecting on your strengths, weaknesses and accomplishments, always seeing the good in it all. Identify areas of your physicality and personality that make you unique as an individual, and identify areas that you can work on improving. You can also create a list of the qualities and skills that you are proud of, and revisit it regularly. Acknowledge your positive traits and achievements without downplaying them, but also remain open to constructive feedback. This balance of self-assurance and humility ensures that your confidence uplifts rather than intimidates others.

Faith can also play a transformative role in building confidence. As 2 Timothy 1:7 reminds us, *"For God has not given us a spirit of fear, but of power and of love and of a sound mind"* (NKJV). Let this verse be a source of encouragement as you step into new opportunities and challenges, knowing that you are divinely equipped to succeed. You *must* believe that you are capable of achieving whatever you put your mind to, knowing without a doubt that God will help you to succeed when you trust Him.

Diamonds are Forever: Know Your Value and Your Worth

Imagine a diamond—a symbol of beauty, strength, and resilience. A diamond's value does not diminish because it is hidden or because someone fails to appreciate its brilliance. I like to remind my students that diamonds are found deep beneath the earth's surface, and become beautifully brilliant through a process of refining. They are not common stones, as those found on the surface, but are highly valuable in their worth because of the great effort that must be put into finding them and refining them. Similarly, *you* are not common. From now own I want you to see yourself as a diamond, knowing that your worth is great, and is not determined by external validation or the opinions of others. Recognising your value is an essential step toward building unshakable confidence.

To understand your worth, begin by acknowledging that you are fearfully and wonderfully made. As Psalm 139:14 declares: *"I will praise You, for I am fearfully and wonderfully made; marvellous are Your works, and that my soul knows very well"* (NKJV). This truth serves as a reminder that you are uniquely created with purpose and significance. Your talents, experiences, and even your trials contribute to the person you are today, making you irreplaceable.

Embracing your worth involves investing in yourself. Just as a diamond is refined through meticulous care, so too must you put effort into your own personal growth. Pursue activities that enrich your mind, body, and spirit, whether it's taking a course, engaging in physical fitness, or spending quiet time in prayer and reflection. Surround yourself with people who affirm and support your journey. Let go of relationships or environments that diminish your sense of self-worth, knowing that you deserve to be treated with respect and kindness.

When faced with criticism or rejection, hold onto the truth of your value. Remember, a diamond's worth does not decrease because someone fails to recognise it. Similarly, your worth remains constant, regardless of external circumstances. This mindset empowers you to navigate life with grace and resilience, secure in the knowledge of who you are.

Overcoming Fear and Self-Doubt

Fear and self-doubt are common hurdles on the journey to confidence. They often manifest as a critical inner voice, doubtfully questioning your abilities or amplifying your weaknesses and shortcomings. While these feelings can be debilitating, they are not insurmountable. By addressing them head-on, you can transform fear into courage and self-doubt into self-belief.

Start by identifying the sources of your fears. Are they rooted in past experiences, societal expectations, hidden insecurities, or your own perfectionism? Write them down. Once you understand their origins, challenge these fears with truth. For instance, if you're hesitant to take on a leadership role because you fear failure, remind yourself that every great leader has faced setbacks. They did not shrink back from their passion and purpose, but persevered despite their challenges. So can you. Know that failure is not the opposite of success but a stepping stone toward growth. Instead, don't anticipate failure, but believe for success. Remember the lesson on the elegant mindset earlier? Review it if you need to, but it is important to be aware of your thoughts. If you expect to fail, then you've failed already. Focus on achieving success, and should failure come, learn from that experience and try again. Failure is only final if *you* decide that it is.

Faith is a powerful antidote to fear. Scripture offers countless reminders of God's presence and provision in times of uncertainty. Reflect on Isaiah 41:10, which says: *"Fear not, for I am with you; be not dismayed, for*

I am your God. I will strengthen you, yes, I will help you, I will uphold you with My righteous right hand" (NKJV). Let this promise give you the courage to step out of your comfort zone, trusting that God is with you, and you are never alone.

Practical steps can also help you overcome self-doubt. Set achievable goals and celebrate each milestone, no matter how small. Surround yourself with positive influences, whether it's mentors, friends, or inspirational books, and fill your mind daily with positive, uplifting things. Engage in activities that challenge you, such as public speaking or learning a new skill. Each experience builds your confidence, reinforcing the belief that you are capable of more than you realise.

How to Overcome Rejection

Rejection can feel like a personal affront, shaking your confidence and leaving you questioning your worth. It can really have you wondering, *"Am I good enough?"*. Yet, rejection is an inevitable part of life and can be a powerful teacher if approached with the right mindset. An elegant woman views rejection *not* as a reflection of her value but as a *redirection* toward something better.

Consider the story of J.K. Rowling, who faced numerous rejections before her Harry Potter series became a global phenomenon. Her perseverance serves as a testament to the importance of resilience. Rejection does not define you; it is merely one person's opinion or one missed opportunity in a world filled with possibilities.

To handle rejection with grace, allow yourself to feel the disappointment but resist the urge to dwell on it. Use the experience as an opportunity for self-reflection. What can you learn from the situation? How can you grow or improve? What can you do differently? Journaling can be a helpful tool for processing these questions and gaining clarity.

Remember, rejection often has little to do with your worth and more to do with circumstances beyond your control. By re-framing rejection as a stepping stone rather than a stumbling block, you maintain your confidence and continue moving forward.

Grace Under Pressure: Confidence in Action

Confidence is most evident in how you handle life's challenges. Whether it's a high-stakes presentation, a difficult conversation, or an unexpected setback, your ability to remain composed reflects your inner strength and poise.

Poise and preparation are essential for demonstrating confidence under pressure. Before a challenging situation, take time to prepare mentally and emotionally. Practise deep breathing exercises to centre yourself and visualise a positive outcome. Think, *"what's the best that can happen?"*, then see it in your mind. If you're speaking publicly, rehearse your key points and anticipate potential questions. By equipping yourself in advance, you reduce anxiety and enhance your ability to respond thoughtfully.

Grace under pressure also involves staying true to your values. When faced with criticism or conflict, resist the urge to react defensively. Instead, listen actively, acknowledge others' perspectives, and respond with kindness and clarity. This approach not only diffuses tension but also elevates your presence, leaving a lasting impression of elegance.

Practical Exercises to Build Confidence

1. **Affirm Your Worth:** Write a list of affirmations, such as "I am capable," "I am loved," and "I am worthy." Repeat

them daily to reinforce your confidence.

2. **Embrace Small Wins:** Set achievable goals and celebrate your progress, no matter how minor. Each success builds momentum and self-belief.

3. **Role-Playing Scenarios:** Practise responding to challenging situations, such as interviews or conflicts, with a trusted friend. This builds your confidence in real-life scenarios.

4. **Reflect on Scripture:** Meditate on verses like Philippians 4:13—*"I can do all things through Christ who strengthens me"* (NKJV). Let this guide and encourage you.

5. **Serve Others:** Engage in acts of service, such as volunteering or mentoring. Helping others fosters

gratitude and reinforces your sense of purpose.

By cultivating authentic confidence, embracing your worth, and overcoming fear and rejection, you become a woman of elegance and strength. Confidence is not about perfection but about embracing who you are and trusting in the path God has laid before you.

Chapter 4

Strengthening

Emotional Intelligence

Chapter 4:

Strengthening Emotional Intelligence

Understanding Your Emotions: The Key to Inner Peace

Emotions are reactions that humans experience in response to events or situations, whether mentally or physiologically, which in turn, affect our thinking and behaviour. Emotions influence our decision-making, daily activities and relationships, and understanding them can help us to navigate life more effectively. Many women commonly struggle to manage their emotions, often allowing these emotions to dictate their reactions and behaviour. If we are not aware of our emotional states, then we may say or do some things that we may later regret, whether with loved ones, friends, work colleagues or even complete strangers.

Some examples of emotions are: (positive) happiness or joy, love, surprise, excitement, encouragement or inspiration, peace, triumph; (negative) sadness, anger, fear, disgust, hatred, bitterness, envy, disappointment, shame, guilt, embarrassment and sympathy.

As elegant women, we *must* develop the skill of effectively regulating our emotions. Most often, emotion regulation is useful in lessening or dampening the intensity of negative emotions, such as anger, disappointment, or fear. A healthy set of emotion regulation skills keeps people from behaving in counterproductive ways when they are emotionally activated. They are especially important for maintaining healthy social relationships.

What is Emotional Intelligence?

"He who is slow to anger is better than the mighty, and he who rules his spirit, than he who captures a city." - Proverbs 16:32.

Emotional Intelligence is defined as, the ability to identify your own emotions and the emotions of others, and use this information to guide behaviour. Strengthening emotional intelligence begins with understanding your own emotions—what they are, why you feel them, and how they impact your life. It's not about suppressing your feelings, but learning to channel them constructively.

Emotional intelligence consists of four key components: *self-awareness, self-management, social awareness, and relationship management.*

Self-awareness is the foundation; it is the ability to recognise and understand your emotions as they arise. This includes noticing what we feel and being able to name it. It also helps us to be honest about our personal strengths and weaknesses. Self-awareness requires that we be observant and introspective. For example, consider the frustration of missing a deadline. Instead of lashing out on the persons nearest to you, or internalising blame, self-awareness allows you to acknowledge your feelings and identify their source. By asking yourself, *"Why do I feel this way?"*, you begin to understand your emotional triggers, which gives you the power to respond thoughtfully rather than react impulsively.

Self-management, the second component, is the art of practising self-control, where we are not ruled by our own feelings, but are instead able to take a step back and make wise decisions. When put into practice, you will be able to exercise thoughtfulness, where you pause and think before you speak or act. You'll also be able to practise restraint, display integrity and readily adapt to change. This doesn't mean suppressing how you feel, but instead, choosing a response that reflects your inner elegance and grace.

Social awareness is the ability to show *empathy*, perceiving the emotions, needs and concerns of the people around you. When put into practice, it enables you to understand why people are the way that they are, and behave the way that they do. It will help you to feel comfortable socially, and even recognize the power dynamics in a group or organisation.

Relationship management is all about having good communication skills. Only when you learn to communicate clearly can you develop and maintain good relationships, (a quality that is highly valuable in elegant women), as well as inspire and influence others positively. This will also enable you to work well in teams and be well equipped to manage conflicts effectively. Let's go a bit deeper now.

Empathy and Compassion: Building Meaningful Connections

How can we truly understand another person's behaviour? We do this through using empathy. Empathy is the ability to step into another person's shoes and see the world from their perspective. An empathetic woman can connect with others on a deeper level, offering understanding and support in times of joy or struggle, because you know how you would feel, if you were in their position. Compassion, which often stems from empathy, goes one step further. It motivates you to act on your understanding, whether through words of encouragement, acts of service, or by simply being present. For instance, imagine a colleague who is visibly upset at work. Empathy allows you to notice and understand their distress, while compassion prompts you to check in and offer help.

Building empathy begins with active listening. People need to feel like they are seen, and they are heard, because they matter to you. When someone speaks, give them your full attention, resist the urge to interrupt or check your phone, and validate their feelings. For example, if a friend shares a personal struggle, you might respond with, *"That sounds really challenging. I'm here for you"*. This simple yet genuine act of acknowledgment can make a world of difference in someone's life.

Not only is compassion important in your relationships with others, but also with yourself. You're going to make mistakes and face setbacks, and that's completely natural. How you face them will have an enormous effect on their outcome. So be sure to extend grace to yourself whenever you do go through such experiences. As Proverbs 31:26 describes the virtuous woman: *"She opens her mouth with wisdom, and on her tongue is the law of kindness"* (NKJV) - both to herself and toward others. Let this verse guide you as you interact with others and yourself, creating an atmosphere of understanding and care.

Facing Conflict with Grace: Elegant Ways to Handle Disagreements

Conflict is an inevitable part of life, but how you handle it defines your character and emotional maturity. An elegant woman approaches disagreements with grace, seeking peaceful resolution as far as possible, without compromising her values or dignity.

The first step in navigating conflict is to *remain calm.* Anger and frustration can cloud your judgment and only escalate tensions. When you feel your emotions rising, take a moment to breathe deeply and collect your thoughts. This pause allows you to approach the situation with clarity and composure. This is where self-management comes in, because you will need to stop and think, before you say or do something you may later regret.

Next, focus on understanding the other person's perspective. Instead of immediately defending your position, ask questions like, *"Can you help me understand where you're coming from?"*. This approach not only diffuses tension but also fosters mutual respect. For example, if a friend criticizes a decision you've made, seeking to understand their concerns can turn a potential argument into a constructive conversation.

It's equally important to express your own feelings and needs assertively yet respectfully. Avoid blaming language, such as *"You always..."* or *"You never...,"* which can put others on the defensive. Instead, use "I" statements, such as *"I feel hurt when..."*

or *"I would appreciate it if..."*. This communication style encourages collaboration rather than confrontation.

Forgiveness is another essential element of handling conflict. Ephesians 4:32 urges us: *"And be kind to one another, tender-hearted, forgiving one another, even as God in Christ forgave you"* (NKJV). Forgiveness is not about condoning wrong behaviour but freeing yourself from the burden of resentment. It will not always be easy, but you *must* let go of past and present offences. By choosing to forgive, you can function from a place of empathy and compassion, and create space for healing and reconciliation to occur.

Finally, set boundaries when necessary. If a relationship or situation continues to cause harm, it's okay to take a step back and operate from a safe distance, while maintaining grace and respect. At the end of the day, we cannot control other people's actions, but we can determine how we allow them to treat us. Prioritising your well-being is not selfish but an act of self-respect and emotional intelligence.

Practical Exercises for Strengthening Emotional Intelligence

1. **Emotion Journal:** At the end of each day, write about moments when you felt strong emotions. Reflect on what triggered them and how you responded. Over time, this practice enhances self-awareness.

2. **Empathy Practice:** Choose a person you interact with regularly and try to see the world through their eyes. Imagine their challenges, joys, and fears.

3. **Conflict Role-Play:** With a trusted friend, practise resolving hypothetical conflicts using calm and respectful language.

4. **Forgiveness Letter:** Write a letter (you don't have to send it) to someone who has hurt you, expressing your feelings and your decision to forgive. This exercise can bring emotional closure.

Strengthening emotional intelligence is an ongoing journey, but the rewards are profound. By understanding your emotions, practising empathy, and handling conflict with grace, you not only elevate your relationships but also deepen your connection to yourself and your faith. Emotional intelligence empowers you to live with peace, purpose, and poise—qualities that define the truly elegant woman.

Chapter 5

Improving Health And Well-Being

Chapter 5:

Improving Health
and Well-Being

The Body as a Temple: Honouring God Through Wellness

Your body is a gift from God, intricately designed to carry you through life's journey. As 1 Corinthians 6:19-20 reminds us: *"Do you not know that your body is the temple of the Holy Spirit who is in you, whom you have from God, and you are not your own? For you were bought at a price; therefore glorify God in your body and in your spirit, which are God's"* (NKJV). Caring for your body is not only a practical necessity but also an act of worship, reflecting gratitude for the life you've been given.

To honour this temple, consider how you treat your physical self daily. Are you nourishing it with wholesome foods, moving it with intention, and providing it with adequate rest? Are you avoiding harmful habits or neglect that can erode your health? Viewing wellness as a spiritual responsibility transforms your approach to self-care.

For example, when preparing meals, think of food not just as sustenance but as a means of fuelling your body to fulfill its divine purpose.

When exercising, frame it as a celebration of what your body can do, rather than as a chore or punishment. This mindset elevates routine health practices into meaningful acts of stewardship.

Nutrition: Fuel for a Vibrant Life

Good nutrition forms the foundation of health and well-being. The foods you consume directly impact your energy levels, mood, and overall vitality. Yet, in today's fast-paced world, it's easy to fall into patterns of convenience over nourishment. Prioritising a balanced, nutrient-rich diet is a powerful way to care for yourself and reflect inner elegance.

Focus on whole, unprocessed foods that provide essential vitamins, minerals, and antioxidants. Fruits and vegetables should be the foundation of your diet. These should be complemented by proteins such as chicken, turkey, fish , lean red meats, and legumes. Include healthy fats, such as olive oil, avocado oil, coconut oil, butter or ghee, and various nuts and nut butters, as well as fatty fish (e.g. tuna, salmon, sardines, and mackerel) which are high in omega-3 fatty acids. Choose complex carbohydrates, such as whole wheat foods, oats, brown rice, ground provisions like potato, sweet potato, cassava, yams and more.

Include various herbs and spices that benefit your immune system, like parsley, rosemary, thyme, turmeric, ginger, garlic, onion, cayenne pepper and cinnamon. For example, a vibrant plate might include baked chicken breast, boiled potato with pak choi (bok choi) cooked with carrots, ginger, garlic, onions and cherry tomatoes, and a drizzle of olive oil. This kind of meal not only nourishes the body but also delights the senses.

Avoid processed foods that provide little to no nutritional value and contain harmful ingredients, such as sausage, bacon, smoked meats, corned beef or spam, boxed or canned meals (e.g. macaroni and cheese, spaghetti and meatballs, soups, etc.), artificial cheeses, cereals and snacks. Consume bread and dairy in moderation, and limit your intake of highly inflammatory foods. These include foods that are high in salt, unhealthy fat and sugar, such as fast foods, fried foods, sweets, pastries, candies and more. Keep in mind that sugar increases cravings for carbohydrates, including more sugar. The more sugar that you consume, the more your body stores its excessive amounts as fat, leading to weight gain, among many other things.

Stay mindful of portion sizes and listen to your body's hunger and satiety cues. Overeating, even on healthy foods, can leave you feeling sluggish, while under-eating deprives your body of the fuel it needs, causing you to then overeat to satisfy those needs. Hydration is equally critical—aim to drink plenty of water throughout the day, limiting sugary drinks and excessive caffeine, which can be counterproductive.

All things considered, for your dietary changes to be successfully maintained in the long run, it is necessary that you have a healthy relationship with food. Avoid the trap of guilt or restriction, which can lead to cycles of deprivation and overindulgence.

Instead, focus on moderation and mindfulness. Enjoy your food. For example, savour a piece of dark chocolate or a slice of cake on occasion, enjoying it without guilt. Remember, health is not about perfection but balance.

The Power of Physical Activity: Strengthening the Body and Mind

Exercise is a powerful tool for enhancing both physical and mental well-being. Regular movement strengthens your muscles and bones, improves cardiovascular health, and boosts energy levels. Beyond the physical benefits, exercise releases endorphins, the body's natural mood elevators, which combat stress and promote a sense of joy. When we neglect to exercise, we increase our risk of developing chronic non-communicable diseases (NCD's), such as Type 2 Diabetes, heart disease, or cancer. It is well documented that women who are overweight and/or obese are at an increased risk for developing an NCD, than those who carry a healthy weight. Regular exercise coupled with balanced nutrition can help us to achieve and maintain a healthy weight, thus improving our overall health, while reducing our risk of disease.

To make exercise a sustainable habit, choose activities that you genuinely enjoy. Whether it's dancing, cycling, hiking, swimming, or a brisk walk through your neighbourhood, the key is consistency. Aim for at least 30 minutes of moderate activity every other day. For example, a morning walk can clear your mind and set a positive tone for the day, while an evening Pilates session can help you unwind and reflect. Know that this won't be easy at first. You will have days when you do not feel like exercising, but you must bring yourself to do it out of discipline. It's okay if you go off track sometimes, but don't ever give up. Tomorrow will be another day to try again. Just keep going.

There is great value in adding some variety in your fitness routine. Incorporating different types of exercise—such as strength training, cardio, and flexibility work—not only keeps things interesting but also ensures a well-rounded approach to fitness. A combination of weightlifting and Pilates, for instance, can build strength and improve posture while enhancing flexibility and balance. Find what works best for you, and faithfully stick with it.

Remember, exercise is not just about achieving a certain physique, but about strengthening resilience and vitality so that you can enjoy life with minimal physical restriction. If machines need to move to prevent them from getting rusty and ceasing up, then how much more does the human body? Approach physical activity as a celebration of what your body can do, focusing on progress rather than perfection.

Rest and Renewal: The Importance of Sleep and Relaxation

Rest is an often-overlooked pillar of health, yet it is essential for the body's restoration and repair. Sleep, in particular, plays a critical role in maintaining cognitive function, emotional balance, and overall well-being. Without adequate rest, even the most disciplined nutrition and exercise habits cannot fully compensate for the weakened immunity that a lack of sufficient sleep causes. Not to mention, it shows in the skin through increased facial wrinkles.

Aim for six to eight hours of quality sleep each night. Create a relaxing bedtime routine that signals to your body it's time to unwind. This might include dimming the lights, reading a calming book, or practising gentle stretches. Avoid stimulants such as caffeine or screens before bed, as they can interfere with your ability to fall asleep. For your bedtime routine to be successful, adopt the habit off shutting down activity by, for example, 8:00pm, giving yourself a two hour window so that you can be in bed by

10:00pm. Give yourself a bedtime and align your activities to suit.

Beyond sleep, incorporate moments of relaxation into your daily life. This might include prayer, meditation, or simply sitting quietly with a cup of tea. These pauses allow you to reset and recharge, enhancing your productivity and focus. For example, five minutes of deep breathing in the middle of a busy day can lower stress levels and improve your mental clarity. It's okay to momentarily disconnect, recharge, then reconnect.

Embrace the biblical wisdom found in Psalm 23, verses 1-3: *"The Lord is my Shepherd; I shall not want. He makes me to lie down in green pastures; He leads me beside the still waters. He restores my soul;"* (NKJV). Trust in God's promise of rest, and let it inspire you to prioritise renewal for both your body and soul.

Mental and Emotional Well-Being: Nurturing Inner Harmony

While physical health often takes centre stage, mental and emotional well-being are equally vital. An elegant woman recognises the importance of cultivating inner harmony, as it directly impacts how she navigates life and interacts with others.

Begin by managing stress effectively. Life's demands can feel overwhelming, but resilience comes from a combination of practical strategies and spiritual grounding. For instance, maintain a schedule that balances work, family, and personal time.

Delegate tasks when possible, and set boundaries when dealing with difficult people to protect your mental health. I must again include that regular physical activity also reduces stress levels in the body and boosts mental health.

You can also build a supportive network of trusted friends and mentors who uplift and encourage you. Share your thoughts and feelings with them, and don't hesitate to seek professional help if needed. Therapy or counselling is not a sign of weakness but a proactive step toward growth and healing.

Scripture offers profound guidance for mental and emotional well-being. Reflect on Isaiah 26:3: *"You will keep him in perfect peace, whose mind is stayed on You, because he trusts in You"* (NKJV). By keeping your thoughts aligned with God and His promises for your life, trusting Him to take care of your every concern, you are able to tap into a sense of peace, knowing that everything is going to be okay.

Practical Steps to Enhance Health and Well-Being

1. **Create a Meal Plan:** Plan your meals for the week, focusing on whole, nutrient-dense foods.

2. **Schedule Exercise:** Block time in your calendar for physical activity, treating it as a non-negotiable appointment.

3. **Set a Sleep Routine:** Establish consistent wake-up and bedtime hours,

even on weekends. Your body will get used to this.

4. **Practise Gratitude:** Write down three things you're grateful for each day.

5. **Connect with God:** Dedicate time daily for prayer, meditation, or Bible study to nourish your spirit.

By improving your health and well-being, you honour both yourself and God. A vibrant, energetic body and a peaceful, focused mind allow you to live with intention and joy. These practices not only enhance the quality of your personal life, but also equip you to positively impact the world around you, helping you to fulfill your divine purpose .

Chapter 6

Practising Good Self-Care

Chapter 6:

Practising Good Self-Care

The Art of Self-Care: A Necessity,

Not a Luxury.

In today's fast-paced world, the concept of self-care is often unknowingly perceived as being indulgent. However, true self-care is so much more than fleeting pleasures or superficial pampering; it is a commitment to nurturing your whole self—body, mind, and spirit—so that you can thrive. For an elegant woman, self-care is not a luxury. It is a necessity that enables her to show up fully in her roles and responsibilities.

Imagine trying to pour water from an empty pitcher; it is an impossible task. Similarly, when you neglect your own needs, you may find it difficult to care for others or perform at your best. Self-care ensures that your "pitcher" remains full, allowing you to give generously without depleting your own resources. This perspective transforms self-care into an act of stewardship, recognising that your well-being is a gift entrusted to you by God. You simply must make the time to take care of yourself.

Begin by acknowledging your needs, whether physical, emotional or spiritual, and making self-care a priority. Create a self-care routine that aligns with your values and lifestyle, treating it as a non-negotiable part of your day. For example, setting aside 30 minutes each morning to spend time with God, have quiet reflection, or go for a brisk walk, can have a profound impact on your mood and energy levels for the entire day.

Emotional Self-Care: Guarding Your Heart and Mind

Proverbs 4:23 advises: *"Guard your heart above all else, for it determines the course of your life "* (NLT). Emotional self-care involves protecting your heart and mind from unnecessary stress, negativity, and toxic influences. It is about creating boundaries that safeguard your peace, and adopting habits that foster emotional resilience. As an elegant woman, use caution by not allowing just anyone or anything into your heart.

Start by assessing the emotional environments you engage in daily. Are your relationships uplifting, or do they drain your energy? Do the people around you bring out the best or the worst in you? Really take a good look at where you are and who you're surrounded by. Choose to surround yourself with people who inspire and encourage you, who build you up, challenge you to grow and celebrate you. On the other hand, gracefully distance yourself from those who perpetuate drama or negativity, like discouraging remarks, harsh criticisms, poor language, crass behaviour or otherwise. While this may be difficult, remember that preserving your emotional health benefits everyone involved in the long run. So it is necessary for you to find the most suitable environment for you to thrive in.

Practising emotional self-care also means allowing yourself to feel and process emotions without judgment. If you're sad, give yourself permission to grieve; if you're angry, explore the reasons behind your frustration. Same goes for if you feel any other sort of emotional overwhelm. Once again, journaling can be an effective tool for processing these feelings and gaining clarity in your thoughts. For example, writing about a stressful situation at work or school may reveal patterns or solutions you had not previously considered.

Additionally, it can be tremendously helpful to engage in activities that bring you joy and relaxation, such as reading, listening to music, or spending time in nature. Get back to enjoying your favourite hobbies, whatever they may be. These moments of pleasure are not frivolous; they are essential for recharging your emotional reserves.

Spiritual Self-Care: Staying Rooted in Faith

An elegant woman understands that her strength and serenity come from a deep connection to her Creator. Spiritual self-care involves nurturing your relationship with God, ensuring that your faith remains the foundation of your life.

Begin by dedicating time each day for prayer, meditation or Bible study. These practices allow you to hear God's voice, seek His guidance, and align your life with His will. For example, starting your day with a devotional can set a positive tone, grounding you in God's promises before the demands of the day arise, so that when they do arise, you are well equipped to handle them.

If this seems like a task that you would rather not do on your own, you don't have to. There are wonderful groups of like-minded people that you can connect with. Try attending a good local church or joining a small ladies' group for a sense of community and spiritual accountability. Surrounding yourself with fellow believers fosters mutual encouragement and growth, helping to reinforce your faith during challenging times. You would also know that when you need help, there will be someone from your support network that can show up for you.

Spiritual self-care also includes surrendering your worries to God. As Philippians 4:6-7 reminds us: *"Be anxious for nothing, but in everything by prayer and supplication, with thanksgiving, let your requests be made known to God; and the peace of God, which surpasses all understanding, will guard your hearts and minds through Christ Jesus"* (NKJV). Trust God with your burdens. He will give you peace to make it through any situation, and this will only strengthen your reliance on Him.

Physical Self-Care: Practising Daily Rituals of Renewal

An elegant woman makes the effort to care for her physical body. From her skin, to her hair, fingernails and even her smile, she puts care into her outward appearance. Physical self-care goes beyond basic personal hygiene. It encompasses activities that maintain and enhance your physical well-being. By treating your body with respect and kindness, you develop a sense of dignity and poise that radiate outwardly.

Start with simple yet impactful rituals. For example, a skincare routine tailored to your specific needs can become a moment of mindfulness and self-appreciation. Another example is, having a daily stretching session in the morning or before bed. This can release tension in your muscles and improve your posture, contributing to an air of elegance in your movement.

Nutrition and hydration are also key components of physical self-care. As we saw earlier, it is necessary that you fuel your body with nourishing foods that sustain energy and vitality, and drink plenty of water throughout the day. For instance, carrying a water bottle with you on the go can help you to remember to drink water and stay well hydrated.

Regular movement is another cornerstone of physical self-care. Whether it's a structured exercise program or spontaneous activities like dancing or gardening, find ways to keep your body active. As seen in the earlier chapter, these practices not only improve your physical health but also boost your mood and confidence.

Finally, prioritise rest and relaxation. Ensure that you're getting enough sleep each night and take breaks when needed during the day. A well-rested body and mind are more resilient, enabling you to face challenges with grace and clarity.

Personal Grooming: Small Details, Big Impact.

Personal grooming is a vital aspect of self-care that enhances your physical appearance and boosts your confidence. Think of it as polishing a diamond—the sparkle is in the details. An elegant woman understands that grooming is not about vanity, but about respectfully presenting her best self with pride and respect for others.

Start by establishing a consistent skincare routine. Cleanse, moisturize, and protect your skin daily with sunscreen. This is for your full body, with special attention given to our face, neck and hands. Moisture and hydration are key for maintaining fresh, youthful-looking skin. Weekly treatments, such as exfoliation or a nourishing mask, can also add an extra layer of care. For example, taking 15 minutes as a part of your bedtime routine, to pamper your skin with a calming face mask can be rejuvenating after a long day.

A woman's hair is her "crown", so it's important that you pay attention to your hair. Ensure that it is clean, well-maintained, and femininely styled to suit your features. Whether you prefer a sleek bun or loose curls, your hairstyle should reflect your personality and complement your overall look. Regular trims, treatments, reduced stress and proper nutrition, prevent hair loss and damage, and keep your hair looking healthy. If you colour your hair, ensure that your roots are touched up, and choose naturally occurring hair colours that complement your complexion. Your hair colour should not grab attention, nor overpower your appearance. Colours like black, shades of brown, natural-looking reds, gold, bronze or blonde are all naturally occurring hair colours. Avoid artificial-looking colours such as blue, fluorescents, pink, green, purple, yellow, orange and the like, as these can take away from a refined, elegant look.

Grooming also includes keeping your fingernails and toenails tidy. Shape your fingernails and opt for neutral tones of nail polish, or a classic French manicure for a polished appearance. If you enjoy colour, choose shades that align with your wardrobe and style, only using natural berry colours like different shades of red or pink for a healthy, feminine look. Avoid unnatural colours like black, grey, blue, green, dark purple, or otherwise, as these may not display the most elegant appearance for your hands. When nail polish becomes chipped or outgrown, either have them redone, or remove the colour completely. Chipped fingernails are never a good look for an elegant lady. Keep fingernails at a reasonable length (not overly long), and be sure to regularly trim your toenails. Taking time to care for your hands and feet communicates attention to detail and respect for yourself.

One of the most attractive parts of a woman's appearance is her smile. Make a special effort to take good care of your teeth. Brush your teeth at least twice per day, and floss daily. If they require straightening, brightening or cleaning in any way, try to make the effort to fix them. Your smile not only enhances your facial features, but also indicates friendliness, confidence and warmth. You'd be amazed by how incredible you feel when you are confident about your smile.

Makeup, when used subtly, enhances your natural beauty. It should not be used as a heavy mask, but as a gentle aid to enhance what's already there. Opt for a look that accentuates your best features—a touch of mascara, gentle eye liner, a soft blush, natural colours of eyeshadow that blend well with your complexion and your attire, and a neutral or berry tone lipstick can create a fresh and polished appearance. Avoid heavy or overly dramatic makeup, as remember, elegance lies in subtlety.

Your wardrobe plays a role in personal grooming. Choose clothing that fits you well, flatters your body shape, and aligns with your values. We'll go a bit deeper into your personal style later on, but know that it's important that you invest in quality clothing over quantity, and select pieces that make you feel confident and comfortable. Ensure that your clothing is clean, well ironed, and free from damage, such as rips, cuts or missing buttons for example. These small details can either elevate or detract from your presence.

Finally, have a signature scent: a unique scent that people remember you by. Perfume is a subtle yet powerful way to leave a lovely lasting impression. Choose a fragrance that resonates with you, opting for floral or fruity scents, and apply it sparingly to pulse points for a gentle, elegant effect. Your scent should not be overpowering, as it may become offensive to others if it's too strong. A simple, pleasant smell that is uniquely yours, is all it takes for you to be well remembered.

The Ripple Effect of Self-Care

When you invest in your well-being, the benefits extend far beyond yourself. Self-care enables you to be more present and effective in your relationships, work, and community. It equips you to serve others from a place of abundance rather than exhaustion, embodying the love and compassion of Christ.

For example, a woman who prioritises her mental and emotional health can approach a difficult conversation with patience and empathy. Similarly, someone who maintains physical vitality can actively participate in her children's lives, creating memories that will last a lifetime. Self-care also serves as a powerful example to those around you. By demonstrating the importance of caring for yourself, you inspire others to do the same. This ripple effect can transform families, workplaces, and communities, fostering a culture of health and harmony.

Practical Steps for Practising Good Self-Care

1. **Set Boundaries:** Learn to say no to commitments that overwhelm you, freeing up time for what truly matters in your life.

2. **Create a Morning Ritual:** Start your day with practices that nurture your mind, body, and spirit, such as prayer, stretching, or journaling.

3. **Prioritise Rest:** Establish a consistent sleep schedule and create a bedtime routine that promotes relaxation.

4. **Connect with Nature:** Spend time outdoors to rejuvenate your spirit and appreciate God's creation.

5. **Reflect on Scripture:** Use verses like Matthew 11:28—*"Come to Me, all you who labour and are heavy laden, and I will give you rest."* (NKJV) as reminders to prioritise renewal.

6. **Refine Your Appearance:** Dedicate time to personal grooming, ensuring that your physical presentation reflects your inner elegance and confidence.

By embracing good self-care, you honour the unique and precious individual who God created you to be. This commitment to yourself is not an act of selfishness. It is a declaration of your worth and a foundation for living a life of elegance and purpose. Through regular self-care, you equip yourself to navigate life's challenges with strength and serenity, becoming a beacon of grace and a positive influence for those around you.

Chapter 7

Physical Elegance –
Style and Presence

Chapter 7:

Physical Elegance - Style and Presence

Dressing the Part:

Modesty with Flattery

Your outward appearance speaks volumes before you utter a single word. The way that you adorn your body and carry yourself gives the world around you a glimpse at how well you value yourself, your level of confidence, your level of sophistication and your personality. It's not about adhering to fleeting trends, but about presenting yourself as someone who values dignity, self-respect, and beauty.

When it comes to fashion, elegance equates to modesty. The way that you cover your body's feminine assets, outwardly displays your sense of inner value. Dressing modestly does not have to sacrifice style. You can be very beautifully styled, yet purposefully covered. This is an art of selecting attire that flatters your unique feminine features, celebrating your beauty without revealing too much. It invites admiration for your confidence and class rather than just your figure. Imagine the allure of a well-tailored dress that fits your body gracefully, complemented by accessories that reflect your personality. Modesty does not mean dull or boring—it means intentional and refined. Think of stateswomen, queens and princesses. Think of the wives and daughters of great men in society. How are they dressed? How do they carry themselves? You my dear, are no different. Let's take a look at how you can refine your appearance.

When building your wardrobe, focus on timeless pieces, that is, clothing that is neither trending nor goes out of style. Choose fabrics and colours that enhance your natural complexion and flatter your body shape. Limit your use of stretchy spandex or jersey material, and clothing that is purposely ripped, cut or torn (e.g. some jeans, skirts, t-shirts and sweaters) as these take away from a polished look. Instead, incorporate shirts, dresses, skirts and trousers that are well tailored, including materials such as linen, satin, polyester and cotton blends. Pastel shades and lighter tones look more elegant, compared to loud, bold colours, such as fluorescent pink, green or yellow, for example. However, simply use your discretion when wearing non-pastel shades, such as fuchsia pink, canary yellow or bright orange. An exception can be made for red, black, navy blue and purple, as these always make a good statement when carried well. For instance, a neutral-toned blazer paired with a well-fitted black skirt can exude professionalism and poise. Incorporate softer fabrics like silk or cashmere for special occasions, adding a touch of luxury to your look and feel.

Avoid wearing clothing that show brand names, logos, or large, bold, printed messages, particularly offensive language or symbols, as these messages tend to reflect your character to the world around you. If however, you must wear clothing with printed messages, ensure that they are not eye-catching, nor off-putting, but tastefully done. Again, don't go chasing every trend just because everyone else is wearing it, because when that season passes, you just may be stuck with clothing that you can no longer wear. Instead, invest in classics like a little black dress, white pants, or a trench coat that never go out of style.

Shoes are an essential component of dressing the part. Elegant footwear completes your outfit while adding an extra layer of sophistication. Opt for neutral or classic colours such as black, beige, or navy blue that pair well with various outfits. Avoid shoes that are overly glitzy, metallic, fluorescent, incandescent, or excessively high in heels. A pair of sleek ballet flats or loafers can offer comfort and style for casual outings, while nude or black pumps (no more than three to four inches high) are ideal for formal settings. For summer, consider strappy sandals with a low heel for a graceful yet relaxed look. Avoid shoes that are excessively worn or scuffed, as they can detract from your overall appearance. Regular maintenance, such as polishing leather shoes or replacing worn soles, ensures they remain polished and well kept. These same guidelines can be applied when choosing handbags and belts.

Accessories play a crucial role in creating a polished look. A pearl necklace, elegant earrings, or a structured handbag can elevate even the simplest outfit. Remember with elegance, less is more, so choose a few key pieces to be worn at a time, rather than overloading with accessories. Gold, silver, pearls and polished stones all add to a high quality look. Wood and shells can also work for the summer or sunny, casual times. Avoid plastic, bulky accessories, as these may tend to cheapen your look.

If you're on a budget, you can still achieve a high quality look using tastefully selected costume jewellery, such as faux gold or silver, pearlesque pieces, high quality solid plastics as gem-like pieces, or crystal pieces. These can still look just as attractive, and speak well for your taste and sense of style. Whether real or faux, an understated yet sophisticated look will always turn heads for the right reasons.

Ribbons and scarves are also quite feminine and stylish, and can be worn in the hair (both), around the neck and shoulders (scarves) or waist (ribbons). Go for lightweight silk, satin or chiffon, in colours that complement your wardrobe. They can add feminine and sometimes girlish flair without overwhelming your outfit.

For cold seasons, a well-fitted coat or trench in neutral tones like camel or grey, adds a touch of refinement to your outerwear. Pair this with leather gloves and a matching handbag for a cohesive, polished look. Remember that your shoes and your handbag should always match in colour. If wearing a belt, then your belt must match them as well.

Elegant Movement: Posture, Presence, and Poise

How you carry yourself is just as important as how you adorn your body. When you've done the inner work and you live with a sense of purpose and identity, secure in who you are as a woman, your confidence emanates from the inside out. Your inner elegance and grace is outwardly shown in your poise and posture, enhancing your physical elegance. A woman who stands tall no matter her height, walks with purpose, and moves with intention commands respect and admiration wherever she goes.

Let's start with posture. Imagine a string pulling you upward from the top of your head. Gently roll your shoulders back, chest slightly forward, and chin parallel to the ground. Keep your back straight. Letting your tummy hang causes your spine to curve forward and your posture to be slouched. Hold your abdomen in, as this helps to keep your back straight. This simple adjustment not only improves your health but also gives you an air of sophistication. Practise walking with a book balanced on your head to perfect your posture. If the book slips, your posture is off, so practise until it becomes second nature for the book to remain in place.

Your gait should be slow, steady, and purposeful - this shows gracefulness. Avoid hurried, rough or clumsy movements, as an elegant lady is never rushed. Even if moving quickly, instead focus on gliding gracefully, with each step deliberate and poised. If you are accustomed to quick, hurried or conversely, sloppy, nonchalant movement, think of the words *"glide softly"* when you walk. Imagine a swan gliding across a lake, or an egret walking through the grass. It will make all the difference, as you will become aware of your movement and adjust your stride to a more graceful one. High heels, when worn, can add elegance to your stride but must be chosen for comfort and confidence. Practise walking in them until your movements are natural and smooth. Use your hips and add a gentle sway to your walk, as a woman's energy is often shown in her hips. Tightness in the hips shows tension and causes some women to walk rather rigidly. Softness in the hips indicates relaxed confidence, and allows the body to move with the rhythm of your hips in your stride, adding to your feminine allure.

Hand gestures should be gentle and controlled, never rough nor harsh. When moving your hands when you speak, think of the the word, *"soft"*. When moving objects or gesturing to others, think, *"soft"*. Remember, you can be soft yet strong. However embracing soft, fluid movement with your hands and arms, enhances your graceful femininity. Avoid fidgeting or exaggerated motions, as they can detract from your presence.

When sitting, smooth your skirt or dress if wearing one, and sit thoughtfully, never plopping down carelessly. Cross your legs at the ankles with your knees together, keeping your back straight. If crossing at the knees, try to slant both legs to the side, for a more elongated look. You can also sit with both feet together, flat on the floor and knees together, either straight upward or slanted diagonally. Small adjustments like these add to your overall elegance.

Elegance on a Budget: Style Without Overspending

Looking elegant doesn't have to mean spending a fortune on expensive items or treatments. With thoughtful planning and creativity, you can assemble a classy wardrobe and grooming routine on a budget. Start by prioritising quality over quantity. Instead of buying numerous low-cost items, invest in a few high-quality essentials that will last for years. Look for sales, thrift stores, and outlet malls to find designer pieces at a fraction of the cost. If you're a woman who's not into brands, but you have an eye for quality designs and products that look just as good as the popular names, then by all means, go ahead and buy what suits you best.

When shopping for clothing, focus on versatile items. A simple black dress, for example, can be styled for both casual and formal occasions with the right accessories. Neutral colours like black, white, navy, and beige allow you to mix and match effortlessly, creating multiple outfits from a few pieces. You can mix and match with various colours and patterns of blouses, jackets, trousers and skirts that reflect your personality and feminine style.

Consider do-it-yourself grooming. With practice, you can achieve salon-worthy nails, hair, and skincare right at home. Invest in basic tools like a tweezer for your eyebrows, nail file, buffer and clippers, nail polish and nail polish remover. Use the most agreeable skin moisturizers like lotions and essential oils, and have quality hair grooming items like a blow dryer, curlers (rollers), combs, brushes and good quality hair care and styling products. There are countless online tutorials that teach everything from manicures to facials to hair-styling techniques. Learn as much as you can and practise on yourself until you find what works for you best. Your body is your canvas. Feel free to explore the best ways to nurture and enhance its appearance that help you to feel confident, healthy and beautiful, without maxing out your budget.

Accessories can also be pocket-friendly. Costume jewellery, scarves, belts and stylish handbags can add flair to your outfits without breaking the bank. The key is to choose items that *look* high-end, but are made from cost-effective materials. Remember, elegance is about how you carry yourself, not the price tag of your wardrobe.

Practical Steps to Achieve Physical Elegance

1. **Wardrobe Audit:** De-clutter your closet, keeping only timeless, flattering pieces that align with your elevated sense of style and values.
2. **Practise Good Posture:** Stand tall and practise graceful movements daily. Use mirrors to assess and improve your poise.
3. **Invest in Accessories:** Select a few high-quality pieces, such as a signature

handbag or versatile jewellery, to complement your outfits.

4. **Shop Smart:** Take advantage of sales, thrift shops, and online resources to build your wardrobe affordably.

Physical elegance is not a superficial pursuit; it is a reflection of the respect that you have for yourself and for those around you. By dressing with intention, maintaining impeccable grooming, and mastering graceful movement, you communicate an unspoken confidence and charm. Remember, the goal is not to impress, but to express who you are—a woman of dignity, beauty, and grace, inwardly as well as outwardly.

Chapter 8

A Faithful Heart – Nurturing Your Relationship with God

Chapter 8:

A Faithful Heart - Nurturing Your Relationship with God

Walking in Faith: Trusting God's Plan

In becoming a more refined woman, we cannot neglect the necessity of strengthening your spirit. Faith forms the strong foundation for an elegant and purposeful life. To walk in faith is to embrace trust in God's divine plan, even when the road ahead is unclear. It is about surrendering your worries, doubts and fears to Him, knowing that His plans are for your good. As Jeremiah 29:11 assures us: *"For I know the thoughts that I think toward you, says the Lord, thoughts of peace and not of evil, to give you a future and a hope"* *(NKJV).*

An elegant woman does not rely solely on her own understanding, but seeks God's guidance in all things (Proverbs 3:5,6). This trust allows her to remain poised, even during trials, because she is anchored in the knowledge that God's timing and purpose are perfect. She knows that she is never alone, and that God *is* on her side. Consider the story of Esther, a Jewish woman who rose to the position of queen in a foreign land under extraordinary circumstances.

When a decree threatened the annihilation of her people, Esther faced a life-altering choice: remain silent and protect her own safety, or risk her life to advocate for her people.

Encouraged by her cousin Mordecai, who reminded her that she may have come to her royal position "for such a time as this" (Esther 4:14), Esther demonstrated immense courage and faith. She called for a three-day fast among the Jews, seeking God's guidance and strength before approaching King Xerxes uninvited—a bold act that could have led to her death. Her trust in God's plan and her willingness to act resulted in the king's favour, the reversal of the decree, and the salvation of her people. Esther's story illustrates the power of faith to overcome fear and accomplish great things. A quality that you can most certainly possess.

Trusting God's plan does not mean that life will be free from challenges. Challenges will surely come your way. Instead, it means that even in the face of adversity, you can find peace and purpose. Embrace each experience as part of a divine design, knowing that God is shaping you for greater things. Look back on some of the challenges that you faced, that were seemingly impossible, that God delivered you from. See where you are today. Remember how good He has been to you, even when you did not know it. Reflecting on past trials can reveal how God could have used them to prepare you for the blessings that you now enjoy, strengthening your faith in Him and your love for Him.

Prayer and Reflection: Tools for Spiritual Growth

How do you develop the ability to trust in God, no matter what comes your way? The answer is this: you must have a solid relationship with Him. An elegant woman prioritises spending time with her Creator. The only way that you get to know someone is to spend time with them. God is no different in that regard. The more time that you spend with God, the more that you get to know Him and how much He loves you. The more that you know Him, the more you will trust Him. You can spend time with God by reading and meditating on His word (the Bible), and by talking with Him daily through dedicated times of prayer.

Prayer is the lifeline that connects you to God, a powerful dialogue that nurtures your relationship with Him. It is no mere ritual, but an intimate conversation, where you honour Him, pour out your heart, seek His guidance, and express your gratitude. You need not be concerned about using fancy words or outward displays - all that God requires is your humble heart. Come to Him with true sincerity, believing in Him, and He will hear you and answer you. As Jesus said in Mark 11:24, *"Therefore I tell you, whatever you ask in prayer, believe that you have received it, and it will be yours"* (NKJV).

Begin your day with prayer to centre your heart and mind in God's presence. Thank Him for His blessings, seek wisdom for the challenges ahead, and surrender your plans into His hands. Evening prayers provide an opportunity to reflect on the day, express gratitude, and seek forgiveness for any shortcomings.

Incorporating reflective practices alongside prayer can deepen your spiritual growth. Journaling your prayers and reflections allows you to track God's faithfulness over time. For instance, writing about a particular struggle and later documenting its resolution can remind you of His provision, protection and grace.

Meditating on Scripture is another powerful tool. Choose verses that resonate with you and contemplate their meaning and application in your life. For example, Psalm 46:10—*"Be still, and know that I am God"*—invites you to pause amid life's busyness and rest in His sovereignty. Regularly dedicating time to reflection strengthens your spiritual muscles, enabling you to face challenges with grace and confidence, remembering that God is always with you.

Graceful Influence: Living as a Christian Example

An elegant woman is not only transformed by her faith but also becomes a beacon of light to others, through her faith. Her actions, words, and presence reflect Christ's love, inspiring those around her to want to get to know Him also. Jesus reminds us in Matthew 5:16 to, *"Let your light so shine before men, that they may see your good works and glorify your Father in heaven"* *(NKJV).*

Living as a Christian example means embodying love, grace, humility, and compassion in your daily interactions. When faced with rudeness or injustice, respond with kindness and patience, demonstrating the love of Christ. For instance, instead of retaliating against a coworker's negative criticism, you could offer encouragement and seek common ground. Such responses not only diffuse tension but also reveal the strength of your character.

Acts of service are another way to live out your faith. Faith requires action, as it is just as important to demonstrate your belief as much as it is to hold it in your heart (James 2:14-26). The more that you grow in your relationship with God, with easier it will become for you to hear His voice and be led by His Spirit. When you sense Him leading you to do something, through faith, you should obey that leading and do it. Volunteer at your local church, support a friend in need, help a stranger, or simply offer a listening ear to someone who is struggling. However He leads you, know that these meaningful gestures create ripples of positivity, reflecting God's love in tangible ways.

Your faith also equips you to uplift and inspire others. Share your testimony when appropriate, illustrating how God has worked in your life. For example, recounting how prayer provided clarity during a difficult decision can encourage someone facing similar uncertainty. Use your platform—whether at home, work, or in your community—to advocate for kindness, integrity, and hope, representing Christ as His daughter, wherever you go.

Strength Through Surrender

Through the maturing of your faith, you will learn how natural it will become for you to rely on God's grace. His grace can be understood as the divine ability to do that which on your own, you cannot do. It cannot be earned, but is given by God as a gift, through faith in Jesus Christ. When you feel the pressure of being perfect before God, or you're being hard on yourself whenever you make mistakes, remember that His love for you surpasses any mistakes that you could ever make. Embrace your imperfections as opportunities to rely on His strength. As 2 Corinthians 12:9 declares: *"My grace is sufficient for you, for My strength is made perfect in weakness" (NKJV)*. It is in your weakness that God shows Himself strong, to carry through your trials as only He can.

This perspective liberates you from the pressure to control every aspect of your life, allowing you to rest in His care.

When challenges arise, remind yourself that God's plan is greater than your understanding. Trusting in His wisdom enables you to face difficulties with confidence and composure. For example, if a job opportunity falls through, consider it a redirection rather than a failure. If a friendship ends, see it as the end of a season, where God is preparing to take you into a new season of life, with new people that He will send your way. Always keep this Scripture in your heart, to draw on when you need it: *"And we know that all things work together for good to those who love God, to those who are the called according to His purpose."* - Romans 8:28 (NKJV).

Practical Steps to Nurture a Faithful Heart

1. **Daily Devotion:** Set aside time each morning for prayer and Scripture reading. Starting your day with God strengthens your faith and sets a positive tone.

2. **Gratitude Journal:** Write down three blessings each day to cultivate a heart of thankfulness.

3. **Faith-Based Community:** Join a church group or Bible study for fellowship and spiritual growth.

4. **Memorise Scripture:** Commit key verses to memory for encouragement and guidance during good times and tough times.

5. **Reflective Prayer:** Spend a few minutes each evening reflecting on the day and seeking God's guidance for tomorrow.

6. **Acts of Kindness:** Use your faith to serve others, whether through volunteering or simple gestures of love and support.

By nurturing your relationship with God, you develop a faithful heart that radiates elegance and strength. This spiritual foundation not only enriches your life, but also empowers you to uplift and inspire those around you, becoming a true embodiment of grace in action.

Chapter 9

Feminine Grace and Charm in Action

Chapter 9:

Feminine Grace and Charm in Action

Becoming a Positive Influence in Your Community

Now that you have seen the value of inner growth and outward refinement, it's time to see how you can put them into action. True elegance extends beyond your personal appearance and poise; it also involves making meaningful contributions to the world around you by touching the lives of other people. A woman of grace uses her influence to uplift others, creating a ripple effect of positivity wherever she may be. Imagine a garden, where each act of service is planted as a seed that grows into a flourishing bloom, enhancing the beauty of the whole. That is how impactful your contribution to your community can be.

Making an impact and being a positive influence can start with simple actions, such as mentoring a younger woman, leading Bible study for children at your church's Sunday school, volunteering for a cause close to your heart, or even offering a listening ear to someone in need. These small acts demonstrate compassion and selflessness, qualities that radiate true elegance.

One powerful way to influence your community is through leadership. Whether in your workplace, local organisations, or faith groups, don't be afraid to take on roles that allow you to inspire and guide others. Leadership rooted in grace can be a beautiful thing, because it involves genuinely listening, empathising, and fostering collaboration with other people. It's all about setting an example and being the change that you wish to see, not only with your words but with your actions.

Consider starting or joining initiatives that align with your passions. For example, if you value education, volunteer at a literacy programme, or offer after-school lessons for children or teenage students. If you're passionate about the environment, organise clean-up drives or tree-planting events. If you're passionate about health and well-being, advocate for wellness initiatives in your school, workplace or church. By living out your values, you inspire others to do the same, creating a ripple effect that can transform your community for the better.

The Beauty of Kindness: Acts of Graceful Service

An elegant woman is a kind woman. Kindness softens hardened hearts, heals emotional wounds, builds relational bridges, and leaves an indelible mark on those who experience it. A kind woman is like a gentle rain—nourishing, refreshing, and life-giving. Let kindness flow from the inside of you naturally, and demonstrate it through your acts of service.

Acts of service don't have to be elaborate or time-consuming. A warm smile, a thoughtful compliment, an encouraging word, or holding the door open for someone, are simple yet impactful ways to show kindness. These gestures may seem small, but their effect can be profound on those receiving it. Consider the biblical principle: *"Do unto others as you would have them do unto you"* *(Luke 6:31, NKJV).* This Golden Rule is a guide for living a life of grace. When you extend kindness without expecting anything in return, and treat people the way that you would like to be treated, you embody the heart of Christ's teachings.

For instance, think of Princess Diana, often referred to as the "People's Princess." Her life was a testament to compassion and service. She was known for her heartfelt dedication to causes like HIV/AIDS awareness, leprosy eradication, and landmine clearance. Diana didn't just lend her name to these causes; she actively participated by visiting hospitals, holding hands with patients, and advocating for those who were often overlooked. Her leadership was rooted in compassion and her ability to connect with people from all walks of life. She once said, *"Carry out a random act of kindness, with no expectation of reward, safe in the knowledge that one day someone might do the same for you"*. Diana's actions demonstrated how kindness and grace could inspire profound change. While you may not have a global platform like she did, you *can* emulate her spirit of service in your own community and daily life. Remember, even a small act of service, when done with love, can make a big difference.

Inspiring Others: How Elegance Transforms the World

Let's extend our scope even further, looking at the impact of elegance on the global community. Far beyond personal pursuits, elegance has the power to inspire and uplift others from all walks of life even beyond borders. You can be a woman who embodies grace and charm, becoming a beacon of light in a world that often feels chaotic and unkind. Because of who you are, what you believe and how you live your life, your very presence can encourage others to embrace their own potential for beauty, kindness, and strength.

One inspiring example of elegance in action is Audrey Hepburn. Known for her timeless style and grace, she also dedicated much of her life to humanitarian work as a UNICEF Goodwill Ambassador. Hepburn's ability to use her platform for the greater good serves as a reminder that elegance is not about self-promotion but about making a difference in other people's lives.

To inspire others, simply live authentically and consistently. Do what you feel called to do, do it well and don't stop doing it. Whether it's a talent or skill, business, charity or otherwise, just stay consistent. Work at it daily, not to impress anyone, nor to gain their attention or applause, but because you genuinely love what you do and believe in its cause. People are drawn to individuals who are genuine and steadfast in their values.

If you are not able to find groups of people to connect with, then you can create opportunities to share your journey. Host workshops, lead discussion groups, or write about your experiences. Sharing your insights and challenges makes you relatable, and shows that elegance is a journey, not a destination.

Along the way, it's important to pause and celebrate the achievements of the people around you, especially other women. Acknowledge their efforts, offer words of encouragement, and help them to see their potential. Your support can be the catalyst they need to get up and pursue their goals with faith, confidence and grace.

Practical Steps for Living and Leading with Grace

1. **Identify Your Strengths:** Reflect on your unique gifts and how they can be used to serve and inspire others. What can you do, that no one can take away from you?

2. **Foster Relationships:** Build connections based on trust, empathy, and shared goals.

3. **Practise Active Listening:** Make a conscious effort to understand others before offering solutions.

4. **Model Elegance in Leadership:** Lead by example, embodying the values you wish to see in others.

5. **Empower and Uplift:** Provide opportunities for growth, and celebrate the successes of those you lead.

6. **Stay Composed:** Maintain grace under pressure, ensuring that your actions inspire confidence and respect.

Feminine grace and charm, when channelled through leadership, can create lasting change in the lives of others. By leading with empathy, confidence, and humility, you inspire those around you to strive for excellence and grace themselves. Let *your* example leave a legacy of positivity and transformation in other people's lives.

Chapter 10

Leaving Your Mark – The Power of Feminine Leadership

Chapter 10:

Leaving Your Mark - The Power of Feminine Leadership

Qualities of the Feminine Leader

Every woman, whether she realises it or not, has the capacity to lead. The *way* that she leads, however, is what makes the difference between the unrefined, possibly masculine woman, and the elegant, emotionally mature woman. This is because feminine leadership is not about authority or control, but about inspiring and empowering others through empathy, strength, and authenticity.

Consider Florence Nightingale, the founder of modern nursing. Known as "The Lady with the Lamp," she transformed healthcare through her relentless dedication and innovative reforms. Nightingale's leadership, rooted in compassion and a tireless pursuit of excellence, saved countless lives and inspired generations to serve others selflessly. She once said, *"I attribute my success to this: I never gave or took any excuse"*. Her story reminds us that determination, humility, and service are the hallmarks of true leadership.

Leadership begins with self-confidence, balanced by humility. You have to believe in your ability to lead others towards whatever your vision may be, within your sphere of influence. There are many ways to do this well. Firstly, an elegant leader makes others feel seen, heard and respected, by listening attentively to their opinions, valuing diverse perspectives, and fostering collaboration between different personalities and groups. This is known as *active listening*. Instead of rushing to offer solutions, take the time to understand the needs, concerns, and aspirations of those you lead. This approach not only makes others feel valued, but also helps you make informed decisions.

For example, in a workplace setting, a woman who mentors her colleagues and encourages open dialogue between them, sets the tone for a harmonious and productive work environment. Her leadership style reflects her values, earning respect and admiration from her team. As a confident yet humble leader, you make every effort to avoid becoming arrogant; instead, let your actions and words reflect your competence. For example, when addressing a team, speak clearly and with assurance, but also encourage feedback and collaboration. This inclusivity strengthens bonds and fosters a sense of shared purpose.

Know that to lead effectively, self-awareness is also an important quality to possess. Make the effort to identify your strengths and weaknesses, and embrace them with humility. A leader who understands herself, is better equipped to understand others. This authenticity fosters *trust*, a cornerstone of effective leadership.

Practical leadership extends beyond professional spaces. As an elegant woman, you can lead within your community, school, church, family, or social circles. You may organise charity events, become the founder of a non-governmental organisation, or advocate for meaningful causes within your society. Imagine a woman initiating a literacy program in her neighborhood, empowering others with the gift of knowledge. Her efforts create a ripple effect, inspiring others to contribute to positive change. Whatever you feel passionate about, don't hold it back, or keep it to yourself. There are people waiting to receive what *only you* have the ability to offer them. Take the time to review the chapter on developing an elegant mind, because this is exactly how you can put it to good use.

To lead with grace, it's important that you embody the qualities you wish to instill in others—integrity, kindness, and perseverance. You have to practise what you preach and be a living example to them, because the people who follow you will emulate your actions and behaviour. If you value punctuality, be the first to arrive. If kindness is your guiding principle, show compassion in your actions. Your behaviour sets the tone for those you lead, demonstrating that elegance and effectiveness go hand in hand.

When your followers become inspired by your good example, they will go above and beyond to not only become the best that they can be, but to also support your vision so that your cause is successful. Remember that leadership is not about commanding attention or dominating others, but about inspiring action and instilling hope in the hearts and minds of your followers. It is about leaving others better than you found them, creating a legacy of impact and influence.

Therefore, empower the ones who follow and look up to you. A true leader sees the capacity for greatness in those she leads, and draws it out of them by lifting them and helping them discover and reach their greatest potential. You can do this by delegating tasks thoughtfully, providing constructive feedback, and celebrating achievements, no matter how small. By creating an environment where others can thrive, you magnify your impact as a leader.

Building a Legacy of Grace and Strength

What is your legacy? When you leave a place, how do you want to be remembered? Legacy is the culmination of a life well-lived. It is defined not by material achievements but by the values and memories you leave behind, even for generations to come. Your legacy is the imprint of your character, the inspiration of your actions, and the wisdom you impart to others. It is the testament that says that you were here, and that you made a difference.

How can you etch your name into history? Start by building a legacy, and building a legacy begins with living each day intentionally. Begin by identifying your core values and ensure that your daily actions reflect them. You must live out what you believe, standing unwaveringly in your faith. If kindness and generosity resonate with you, find ways to express these traits consistently, because it is by your consistency that you will be known and remembered.

Consider Deborah, one of the most remarkable women in the Bible, whose story exemplifies the power of leadership, wisdom, and faith. Deborah was a prophetess and judge in Israel during a time of turmoil and oppression. She not only administered justice with fairness but also provided spiritual and military leadership to Israel's army. Under her guidance, Barak, Israel's military leader, led the Israelites to victory against their enemies, and Deborah's song of triumph stands as a testament to her unwavering faith and confidence in God's deliverance (Judges 5).

Deborah's legacy extended far beyond her immediate impact on Israel's freedom. Her legacy is an enduring example of feminine strength and grace. She led with conviction, wisdom, and humility, embodying what it means to inspire others through courage and purpose. Let her story encourage you to embrace your God-given gifts and use them to effect meaningful change in your sphere of influence.

Your legacy is also reflected in the lives of those you influence. Sharing your experiences, lessons, and values with the next generation ensures that your impact endures. For example, starting a blog, teaching classes or writing a book passes on your knowledge to an innumerable number of people for years to come, with an impact that goes far beyond what you could imagine. Creating tangible memories can also preserve your legacy. Documenting your life's journey through journals, photo albums, or video recorded stories allows your loved ones to connect with your experiences and insights. These keepsakes become cherished reminders of your life's journey and the values you held dear.

A legacy of grace and strength is built through consistent effort, intentional actions, and a deep understanding of what truly matters. It is about creating a life that inspires others to embrace their own journey with elegance and true sense of purpose. So don't be afraid to leave your mark in this world, and an unforgettable mark on the lives of others, through the example of being who you are and your unforgettable actions.

Practical Steps for Crafting Your Legacy

1. **Define Your Values:** Reflect on the principles that are most important to you and align your actions accordingly. Let these values guide your decisions and interactions.

2. **Inspire Others:** Use your experiences and insights to mentor and uplift others. Share your journey to encourage others to pursue their goals with confidence.

3. **Contribute Actively:** Engage in causes or projects that reflect your

passions and leave a positive impact on your community.

4. **Preserve Your Story:** Write letters, keep a journal, or create a scrapbook to document your thoughts, achievements, and lessons learned for future generations.

5. **Celebrate Life's Moments:** Appreciate the beauty of everyday experiences, creating memories that will endure in the hearts of those you love.

6. **Lead by Example:** Demonstrate the qualities you value, such as kindness, resilience, and authenticity, inspiring others through your actions.

The legacy of an elegant woman is not confined to a single achievement but is woven through the tapestry of her life. By embracing growth, leading with grace, and living intentionally, you create a lasting impact that inspires others to follow in your footsteps.

Remember, your legacy is a reflection of who you are at your core. Through elegance, authenticity, and strength, you leave behind a timeless gift that resonates far beyond your lifetime. So live with purpose, lead with compassion, and leave a legacy of grace and strength that will inspire generations to come.

Final Words

Final Words:

Embrace the Journey of True Elegance

As you've come to the end of this book, let us remember that true elegance is not a final destination. It is a continuous journey of growth, self-discovery, and outer as well as inner refinement. The principles explored here — embracing your femininity, developing emotional intelligence, practising grace and kindness, nurturing your health and well-being, deepening your faith, and presenting yourself with poise—are more than mere ideals. They are foundational truths that can transform your life when fully embraced.

Elegance begins in the heart. It is reflected in the quiet strength you carry during challenges, the warmth you extend to others, and the unwavering dignity you uphold in all circumstances. It is in the way you choose to rise above negativity, honour your commitments, and inspire those around you with compassion and wisdom. Elegance is the courage to be authentic, the humility to keep learning, and the faith to walk with purpose.

This journey requires consistency. Some days will feel easier than others, yet it is in those moments of struggle where your character is truly refined. When you stumble, extend yourself grace and rise again with greater strength. When you feel unseen, remember that true elegance needs no audience—it flourishes in quiet moments of integrity and inner growth.

As you continue to develop the values of kindness, humility, godliness, and self-respect, you will find that elegance becomes a natural extension of who you are. It will influence how you lead, how you love, and how you impact the world around you. Your presence will become a light that encourages others to seek beauty, truth, and goodness within their own lives.

You my dear, were created with purpose. You were designed to radiate grace and strength in every season of your life. Be encouraged to embrace the fullness of your femininity, hold fast to your values, and continue to walk this path of elegance with courage and faith.

May your life be a reflection of the beauty that comes from within—a beauty that inspires, uplifts, and leaves a lasting legacy. This is not the end of your journey. It is only the beginning of becoming the woman you were always meant to be.

About the Author

Leah Lewis is the founder and principal of *The Diamond School of Elegance and Chivalry* - a premier finishing school based in her home country, Trinidad and Tobago. She trains dozens of men, women and young persons in the areas of elegance, social etiquette and personal development, and has witnessed remarkable transformations in her students' lives. Leah is also a Christian author, having penned the book, *"The Lifestyle of Worship - Out of the World and Into the Kingdom"*. She is a public health professional, educator, singer, and former model. Leah is dedicated to instilling the timeless values of grace, sophistication and character in the hearts and minds of many around the world.

To contact the author, please send an email to:

thediamondschool.info@gmail.com

Call or send a WhatsApp message to: +1-868-775-1900.

For more information on her institution, please find *The Diamond School of Elegance and Chivalry* on Facebook or Instagram.

Elegance
from

Within

UNLOCKING THE SECRETS

TO

GRACEFUL FEMININITY

By: LEAH LEWIS

Made in the USA
Las Vegas, NV
15 March 2025